Pearls of ☺
Wisdom

51 Stories To Live Life Ethically

J.M. Mehta

I0112107

V&S PUBLISHERS

Published by:

V&S PUBLISHERS

F-2/16, Ansari Road, Daryaganj, New Delhi-110002
☎ 011-23240026, 011-23240027 • *Fax:* 011-23240028
Email: info@vspublishers.com • *Website:* www.vspublishers.com

Branch : Hyderabad
5-1-707/1, Brij Bhawan (Beside Central Bank of India Lane)
Bank Street, Koti, Hyderabad - 500 095
☎ 040-24737290
E-mail: vspublishershyd@gmail.com

Branch Office : Mumbai
Jaywant Industrial Estate, 2nd Floor–222, Tardeo Road
Opposite Sobo Central Mall, Mumbai – 400 034
☎ 022-23510736
E-mail: vspublishersmum@gmail.com

Follow us on: t f in

All books available at **www.vspublishers.com**

Printed at: Repro Knowledgecast Ltd., Thane.

Publisher's Note

*I*t's often said that Values, Morals and Ethics are intricately tied together. Values are what we learn from childhood; Morals are the intrinsic beliefs developed over our lifespan and Ethics are how we actually behave in various situations that test our moral fibre. Hence, imbibing the right values in life is a must for everyone, who seeks happiness and bliss.

It is true that in our busy life schedule, we hardly get time to think and understand the significance of values, such as honesty, sincerity, faith, kindness, etc. Nonetheless, these values form the basis of our lives, families or the society, as a whole. We can inculcate these values by keeping a good company or by reading some good books teaching us the right values and morals of life for becoming a good person.

The book, *51 Stories to Live Life Ethically*, is a collection of such value-based stories in which each story teaches us some good value of life, as mentioned above through a short and interesting incident which we can easily relate to our day to day life. The language used in the book is simple and lucid, and thus it can enlighten people of almost all age groups.

We hope you enjoy reading these fascinating stories, and learn from them the values that can bring happiness into your life…

Contents

1. Alexander and the Saint

The Broken Myth of Owning the World!

After conquering many countries, Emperor Alexander invaded India, where he met a naked saint, whose words opened the Conqueror's eyes!

Alexander on seeing the naked saint told him, "You have nothing." The saint laughed and said: "The whole universe is mine. I have it without invading it." Alexander said, "How can anyone win the world without conquering it?" The saint replied: "I have won over the Creator of this world. When I own the creator, the whole creation is mine. The way of my conquest is different from yours. I conquer, not by sword, but by surrendering myself!" Alexander was impressed by this reply and felt very pleased. Alexander said, "I too have conquered the world." In response the saint said, "Just imagine for a while that you are lost deep in a desert and are extremely thirsty. Then I appear before you with a jug of water and offer the same to you for a price. In case, you are about to die for water, how much of your kingdom can you give me for a jug of life saving water."

Alexander replied: "I shall be prepared to give half of my kingdom."

The saint said: "Suppose I do not sell my water at that price." Alexander told that he would be ready to give his whole kingdom to save his life. The saint laughed and said: "Then, in that case, only one jug of water is the price of your whole kingdom for which you have wasted your entire life."

These words of the saint had great impact on the mind of Alexander that he gave up the idea of further conquests. This incident which changed his thinking was also one of the reasons which prompted him to return to his country.

2. The Light of Devotion

Difference between pretence and serious work will show up any day!

In order to show off their love and respect to Lord Buddha, rich devotees used to light costly lamps as offerings to him. A very poor woman, who had great love and respect for Buddha, noticed this and she too wanted to offer a lamp, but was too poor to buy one.

Nevertheless, she worked hard, begged and raised a small amount to buy an earthen lamp and filled it with some oil and small cotton wick. She prayed earnestly and begged Buddha to accept her humble offering. Next morning, it came to the notice of one of the chief disciples of lord Buddha that barring a little earthen lamp, all other lamps were extinguished. The little earthen lamp was still burning and was full of oil and wick. He communicated this strange happening to the Lord, who said, "This lamp is lit with the wick of devotion and the oil of sincerity. Nothing will put out this light. Let us all bestow our inner selves with this type of light."

Here, the light is the symbol of inner peace, love and devotion. And all human beings should fill their inner self with light like this.

3. Unselfish Love

The Milk of Human kindness knows no barriers and animals are no exception!

This is a touching story of a very kind person who bought two pups for a distant relative who lived in far off city. He carried the pups by train to deliver them to his relative.

On his way to the relative's house, after getting down from the train in a hired taxi, he asked the driver to halt at a roadside *dhaba* (eatery) to feed the pups with some milk. The taxi stopped in front of a hut which was a small *dhaba*. The gentleman asked the owner for some milk for the pups. An old woman came out and picked up the pups with great love and fed them fondly with milk in a bowl. She told the man that she too had two pups but they were killed by a careless driver on the roadside. The old woman showered all the love and affection on the two pups even though they did not belong to her. Admiring her kind attitude, the man was greatly surprised at the conduct of the poorly dressed old woman and offered her money for the milk. She did not accept the money, washed the pups, kissed them and gave them to the owner reluctantly. She said, "Sir, they also have life, never be cruel to them." There were tears in her eyes when she said these words and looked at the pups with great love as the man took them away. The love and affection that old woman showered on the pups, was like the love from a mother's heart for her own children, untainted and unselfish!

4. A Memorable Gift

Patience is a shield against future regrets!

A young man was very fond of a sports car, exhibited in a dealer's showroom, and told his rich father about it. What followed can be interesting....

At his graduation, the young man expected his father to gift that car to him. On the morning of his graduation, his father called him and gave

his son a gift box. When the son opened it, he found a holy book inside. Angrily he shouted, "With all your riches, you give me just a book!" and left the house and the book.

After several years, the young man became a rich businessman. He realised that he must get back to his father, who had grown old. Just then, he received a telegram informing him of his father's death. When he returned to his father's house, he came to know that his father had willed him all his property and possessions. As he was searching through important papers, he found the same holy book which his father had gifted him at his graduation. Beneath the book he found an envelope, taped and contained papers for a sports car, with the dealer's name. On the papers, the date of graduation was written, along with words, 'PAID IN FULL' what a surprise!

5. Who is Your Real Friend?

Noble Deeds double up as Friends and Fame in life!

A person was accidentally framed for a crime that he did not commit. He was issued a warrant.

He had three friends and he asked one of them to testify to his innocence as a witness. The friend said, "I cannot move out of this house.

But can help you only from here." He, therefore, had to approach others. The second friend said, "I can come up to the doorway of the court but will not enter the witness box."

The third friend said. "I will speak for you, wherever you want me to come." This is the story of our life. The first is PROPERTY which can hear witness only within the house. The second is RELATIVES who would come till the cemetery. The third friend is one's own virtues and noble deeds which continue to shine even after death and stand witness for a long time to come.

The good thoughts and actions of life
will serve as good friends who will
bring peace and progress.

6. The Right Medicine

Solutions stand disguised in the problem itself!

A very fat lady, having problems in walking, decided to consult a doctor to get medication to reduce her fat. The doctor asked her a few questions and told her to come after two days so that he could consult his books and give her the right medicine.

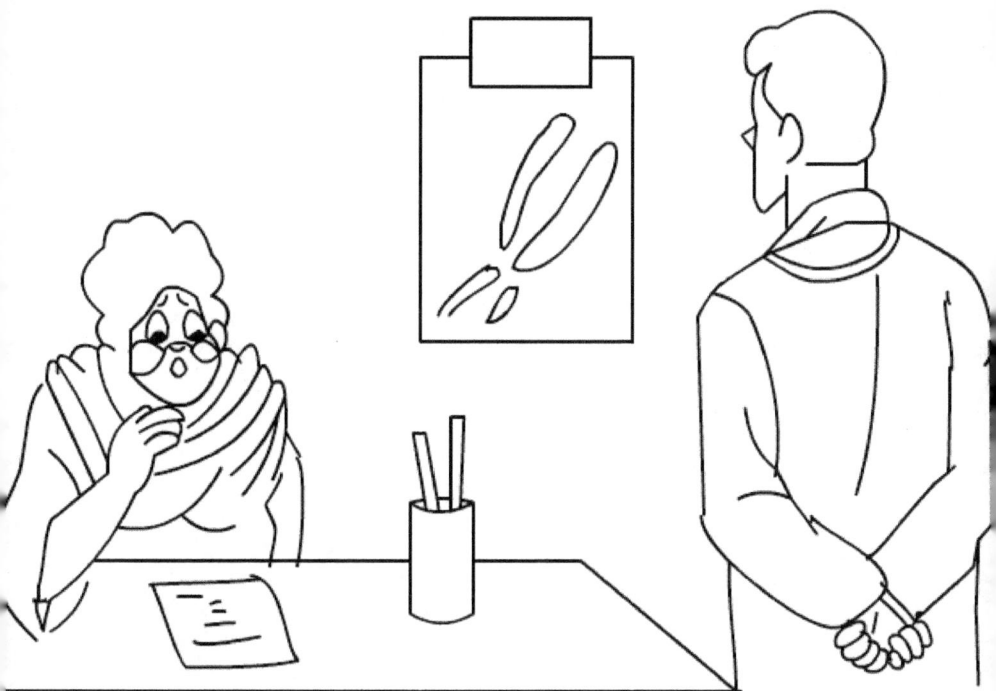

The lady came after two days and the doctor told her, "Madam, I have consulted my books and have come to the conclusion that you will die in the next ten days. Therefore, there is no use giving you any medicine!" The woman got scared and went home. She was very sad and stopped eating and drinking. Due to this, in ten days, she lost a lot of weight and became thin. But she did not die so she went to the doctor after ten days to tell him that she was still alive. The doctor asked her, "Are you fat or thin" She replied, "I am thin and lost all my fat because of the fear of dying." The doctor said, "That was the right medicine for you."

The lady went home happy and satisfied.

7. Rich Man vs. Poor Man

Excuse is the alibi of lazy and selfish!

A poor man was struggling to find money to marry off his daughter. So he approached a rich man for some money. Did the rich man help him?

The rich man was reluctant to part with his money so he put him off saying, "I don't have any spare money, now, please come after some days."

So the poor man went away and returned after a few days and repeated his request.

The rich man said, "I have money now, but I do not have my cashier to give it to you. So please come after some days."

The poor man got the hint and went away saying, "I thought a rich man is also a man!"

8. A True Devotee

Ignore the acts of the wicked and jealous and never react in their language!

*E*knath was a true devotee of God. He would go to the temple every day, after taking bath. One day, when he was on the way to the temple, a jealous man spat on his face. Did Eknath reply violently to this act of aggression?

Eknath went back home, took bath and again that person spat on him. In this way, the man continued to soil Eknath one hundred times; Eknath in turn took bath a hundred times and did not say anything to the wicked man. Finally, the wicked person who was ashamed and remorseful sought Eknath's forgiveness. Eknath simply remarked, "God wanted me to take bath a hundred times." He showed no ill will against the man so much so that he finally became the disciple of the holy man. This is how you can win over those who are on the wrong path.

9. The Sinner and the Christ

Assess one's own worth before judging others!

A woman, a bad character and a sinner was brought before Jesus Christ with her hands tied to the back with a furious mob shouting at her. Christ saved her from the angry crowd and showed her a divine path…

The woman was mobbed by the people who wanted to pronounce death punishment on her. Jesus first looked at her and told the crowd, "If

she is not denying acts of sinning then she surely deserves punishment."
At this, the crowd shouted. "Death to her, punish her."

Jesus said. "Yes, she should be punished as per your wish, and so get ready to hit her with five stones each." Everybody picked up stones to hit her. The woman was terrified.

Then Jesus said loudly, "Beware! Only that man will hit her first, who is not a sinner himself! In case any sinner hits her, he will be punished."

Hearing this, the crowd lowered their hands. Tears rolled down the woman's eyes and she looked towards Jesus. The crowd, which was shouting for punishment started retreating with their heads down. Jesus untied the knot and released her. Jesus said: "You are free to go wherever you want. God is all merciful. You can seek his forgiveness for your sins in all sincerity."

The woman was ashamed and cried out in full force as if her sins were being drowned in the flow of tears as regret and repentance! Such was the magic of a saint's compassion!

10. A Man of Courage

Determination dwarfs all handicaps in life!

$\mathcal{A}$ lady commuter was standing at the roadside looking for a cycle-rickshaw. Suddenly, a rickshaw-puller, clad in *kurta pyjama*, appeared and said, "Madam, are you looking for a rickshaw?" The ride in that rickshaw revealed the noble side of that poor man!

She took the rickshaw and found that the man plying it was very alert and careful while plying it unlike many others. She posed a few questions to the man but he was not talking much. There must be a reason to it....

Then the lady noticed that he had no left leg and he was frequently pulling up the *pyjama* from the left side. The lady felt sympathetic and probed more about him. This time he told his story. He was originally a farmer from Bihar, who lost his left leg in an accident. Deciding not to become a burden on his family, he moved to Delhi along with his wife. He hired a rickshaw on a monthly basis and started earning. His wife too started earning as a housemaid. By this time, his wife was pregnant and both wanted to give their child a good education and groom the kid as a responsible citizen. The man shared many such matters with her and that impressed the lady. When her destination was drawing close, seeing the road in bad shape, she offered to get down a little ahead of her house. But this man insisted on dropping her at the gate of her house. The lady admired his good behaviour and courage and paid him well. He thanked the lady and went away happy and smiling.

11. Let us not Imitate Others

The principal mark of a genius is not perfection, but originality!

This is what late Douglas Malloch said:
        If you can't be a pine on the top of the hill
be a scrub in the valley – but be the best little scrub
by the side of the rill;

Be a bush if you can't be a tree.
If you can't be a bush be a bit of the grass,
and some highway some happier make;
if you can't be a muskie then just be a bass-
but the liveliest bass in the lake!

We can't all be captains, we've got to be crew,
there's something for all of us here.
There's big work to do and there's lesser to do,
and the task we must do is the near."

If you can't be a highway then just be a trail,
if you can't be the sun be a star;
it isn't by size that you win or you fail-
Be the best of whatever you are!

Let us not imitate others.
Let us find ourselves and be ourselves.

12. Love of God

his is a story about Prophet Moses, who heard a voice from a shepherd, saying: "Oh God, where are you? How can I stitch your clothes; mend your shoes and offer you milk?" Moses' annoyance at the shepherd's pleadings with the God led to an interesting revelation!

The shepherd's voice was overflowing with love. Moses was greatly surprised to hear all these and took it as blasphemy. He came to the shepherd and said, "How dare you speak like this? Do you think God is human who can drink your milk and get the hair combed by you! Your talk amounts to insulting our religion."

The shepherd became speechless and wondered whether he had said anything wrong! Heartbroken, he wept and apologised to the prophet and went away. Moses felt happy the he had taught a lesson to the fool. Suddenly a voice thundered, "Moses, why did you interfere between me and my child; who authorised you to separate the lover from the beloved. Why did you drive my faithful devotee away from me? I have no need for praises and worship. It is the sincerity of heart that alone interests me." Moses felt humbled and went after the shepherd. He found him meditating by a spring, calm and compassionate. He was truly full of love of God.

13. A Story of Ideal Love

Accepting people as they are develops trust and understanding!

A married couple loved each other intensely. A few months after marriage, the wife read an article on the ways to strengthen marital relations. She wanted to apply that knowledge in her own life. What followed was interesting....

On the basis of that knowledge, she suggested her husband to make a list of all negative points so that they can discuss candidly and sort out differences. The husband had no objection. Next day, the wife brought out her long list and started reading. While reading, she noticed that her husband's eyes were filled with tears!

She asked, "Anything wrong?" He replied, "No, please carry on." The wife read out the list and kept it on the table, saying. "Now, you read out your list and we shall discuss." The husband said, "I don't have any list. I think you are o.k., the way you are. I don't want you to change for my sake." The wife was surprised and impressed by the straightforward answer which reflected his honest and deep love for her and his total acceptance of her. She wept and embraced him.

The husband-wife relationship lasts long on mutual love and understanding.

14. The Lighter Side

Smiles of Happiness and Smiles of Pretence Differ!

*T*hree dead men were brought to the city morgue. All of them died with a smile on their face. The city police wanted to know the reason of the smile. The disclosed reasons may make you smile...

They discovered that each had a separate reason as in the following:-

The first body was that of a miser who died, counting money. He enjoyed his work very much, hence the smile! The second man was a gambler. While gambling, he had a winning hand of a large amount, and died of heart attack.

The third man was struck by lightning. But the sheen on his face was puzzling. It was later found out that he was a POLITICIAN! When he saw the flash of lightning, he thought he was being photographed; so he had to smile!

15. Sympathy - In a Cup of Tea

Genuine Care Speaks!

An old, emaciated man who underwent a bone marrow transplant was lying on a bed, sad and hopeless. His nurse came and said, "Hello, Mr. John, I am your nurse, Lily. Will you like to have some soup?" He refused; but the nurse had other ideas....

The man shook his head and said, "I want to sleep." Later, she came back with medicine which he took and sank back to his pillow. He did not react and the nurse went back with a feeling dejected.

But the nurse did not lose heart. She went to the kitchen, and made two cups of tea, put on a tray and went to his room. She said politely, "Shall l have my tea in your room and also watch the T.V?" He said, "yes, of course," but closed his eyes.

The nurse put on the T.V. and he opened his eyes and began watching the TV. She noticed this and said, "I have an extra cup of tea, if you care to have it." The man reacted favourably and said, "Just half a cup."Then both watched the T.V. in silence. When she was preparing to leave, he asked, "Will you come tomorrow?" she smiled and said, "Yes, I will and have tea with you again." He said, "I like that."

Next day, he had a full cup of tea and toast and looked better. The nurse talked to him and he felt encouraged. The third night he had two cups of tea and told the nurse about his job and the family. On the fourth night, he got out of the bed and sat in a chair. His routine continued as the nurse conversed with him politely and sympathetically. A few days later, he recovered and went back home.

Some months later, when the nurse went for shopping in a store, she heard a booming noise "Lily, it is nice to see you here." He was his old patient in the hospital. He introduced her to his wife and said, "She saved my life with her sweet talk and many cups of tea." He hugged her, thanked her, before parting company. This is how a nurse helped her patient to recover, with sweet conversation, compassion and many cups of tea!

16. The Hidden Power

Never Ignore Premonitions and Intuitions!

I, my wife, and our handicapped child used to go to a neighbouring park on Sundays, where my son would play and enjoy the green grassy environment. We all used to go in a small car and stay at the park for a few hours and then come back home happy. But one day, I had a strange experience....

Once I parked the car outside the forest garden and we all walked inside and sat on a grassy corner. Our small boy played for a while and fell asleep. We strolled in the park and when he woke up, had some refreshments and came to the parking lot. To my surprise, when I searched for the car-key in my pocket, it was missing! It was lost somewhere in and around the park, but where could I look for it in such a big park? Anyway, something goaded me to retrace my steps and go back to the place where we sat; still the key was not traceable. As I was about to turn around, I looked again towards the corner, where we sat. And to my surprise, I saw something shining and that was the key chain and the key. How did I get it when I was about to go away, disappointed!. Some hidden power indeed!

17. Beauty Beneath Ugliness

Poverty Hits only the Body Not the Mind!

An old woman was sitting on a bench in a public park. She looked very miserable – torn clothes; dirty hair and shabby looks. She had a paper-bag with her that carried her belongings. But she was happy with her past and a small boy discovered her kind heart......

Small squirrels would come near her feet and she would throw small pieces of bread which they would catch and run away. At this, she would burst into petty laughter. A woman and her small boy came that way but did not like to sit with her. But the old woman beckoned the boy who was watching her act of feeding the squirrels. He ran to her and both started feeding the small animals and together enjoyed many hearty laughs. Soon the mother also joined them and shared their joy and mirth.

Initially, both mother and her little boy did not like to share the bench with the ugly woman. Now they both sat with her and shared the fun. They discovered her human side as a generous and loving person. It was the beauty beneath the ugliness that attracted them. Appearances can become deceptive, sometimes!

18. The Evil of Poverty

Love for the child and pangs of poverty!

This is the true story of a poor woman who had no option but to sell her baby for a few bucks. It is a message that there are many unfortunate mothers who struggle to feed their precious child!

A poor woman – an orphan, earned her living doing odd jobs. She gave birth to a baby, and was living on the pavement. Driven by poverty and desperation, she did not want to keep the child and looked for someone who could take care of the baby.

She met a childless couple, who were willing to adopt the baby. The deal was struck for Rs. 2000/-. The news of the sale got public soon. People started questioning both the mother and the couple, who denied the sale and said that they had only given the money for food, etc. They had taken the child as a gesture of help and sympathy as otherwise it will not survive! However, the mother confessed having sold the baby since she could not keep it. Later she revealed that someone had promised to marry her, but backed out. She had, therefore, no option but to sell the child.

19. The Hidden Hand of God

Instincts can be pointers to great things in the Future!

*T*his is the story of a farmer's son, whose father led a righteous life. Right from his very childhood, the young boy had been displaying noble qualities despite formal education. In later life, his instincts made him a wise man.......

The farmer's son used to help his father in farming activities. One day, while working in the field, the son saw a large crab, which he picked up and brought home. He kept it in an earthen pot by the side of his bed and slept. By chance, a cobra entered the room and put its head into the pot. The crab caught the head of the snake and bit it hard and crushed it; as a result the cobra died.

On waking up, the young man was surprised to see the sequence of events. Many questions arose in his mind. "Why did I catch the crab and bring it home?" "How did the cobra come inside?, Why did the snake put its head into the pot, etc. It could have indeed bitten me? and so on." In his later life, this thoughtful boy became a YOGI and found answers to all his questions.

20. Justice of Grandson

Sometimes even children teach their ignorant parents!

An old, sick man used to live with his son and family. They used to have their meals together on the same table. But certain changes happened in the household....

In due course, the hands of the old man became weak and shaky and eating became difficult. Sometimes, the food would fall on the table or floor or clothes. His son and the daughter-in-law would get annoyed and

wanted to do something about it. They put a separate small table in the corner of the dining room, for feeding the old man. They also brought a wooden platter for serving the food since he had already broken some plates. The old man would eat his food, sitting in a corner all alone feeling humiliated. Tears would flow down his eyes.

The old man's five-year-old grandson was silently watching the plight of his grandfather. One day the boy was trying to make something out of some wooden scrap when his father asked, "Son, what are you doing?" The boy replied innocently, "I am trying to make a wooden platter for you and Mom, to eat food, when you grow old, like grandfather." The parents were shocked to hear this. They got the message and were full of remorse. Their eyes became moist with tears.

The same evening, they led their father gently to the same dining table, gave him good food and sought his forgiveness. The old man became happy and ate his food with the family as long as he lived. His son and daughter-in-law never showed any irritation if something fell from his shaky hands.

This is how a small child – a grandson got justice for his old grandfather who was being ill-treated by his son and daughter-in-law.

21. A Brother's Concern

Small acts of kindness can save many lives!

A small boy used to sit near a temple and sell flowers and garlands to the devotees. He used to sit from early morning till late night and try his best to sell flowers. There was a touching story behind his urge to sell flowers....

The boy would always approach a lady, who would visit the temple every day and beg her earnestly to buy flowers, but somehow she never did that. The boy would follow her again even when she came out of the temple. Other boys also sold flowers, but this boy was very persistent in selling his wares.

The same lady did not visit the temple for many days. However, she went there after a gap of many months and saw the same boy sitting there. But this time, he did not ask her to buy the flowers. He looked at the lady and did not utter a word. The lady found this strange and went over to him and asked, "Why did not you ask me to buy your flowers?" He replied, "Madam, why should I ask?. You are rich but can't spend ten rupees to buy a garland from me. But now I am not that desperate to sell. My sister was suffering from cancer. I used to sell garlands to buy medicines for her. She passed away a month ago!"

The lady was so overwhelmed that she bought all his flowers. However, she repented that she did not buy any, when the boy was trying very hard to sell it. Time lost never comes back.

Never hesitate to do a good deed.

22. When Lord Krishna Missed the Ghee

When humour drills in more common sense!

This is the story of a maid, Radha and the deity, Lord Krishna. Radha was working as a maid to one lady. After a few years, she got married and had a baby boy. The lady would visit her home regularly to provide some food for the mother and child.

One day, after taking bath, the lady's husband searched for *desighee* to light the lamp for the daily worship (puja) of Lord Krishna. He could not get it and asked his wife about it. She had given the whole packet of *ghee* to Radha, the maidservant for her nourishment. The husband was annoyed. To this she remarked jokingly, "My Radha needs the *ghee* more than your Krishna."

At this, both the husband and wife burst into laughter. Love for fellowmen is equivalent to the love of God. If we do service to the needy, it amounts to service of the Lord.

23. Be Polite, But Firm

Kind words taste like honey!

Harsh and impolite words can lead to hurt feelings and even hard fights. So it is good to be polite while speaking.

Once Bibi Ayesha, the youngest wife of Prophet Muhammad was shouting at someone as he could not complete some work. Prophet Muhammad heard this out and advised his young wife: "Ayesha, Allah has not provided us with a bone in the tongue. This is simply because

we need to talk to people softly and pleasingly." As spoken words have the potential to promote both love and hatred, it is always advisable to be polite.

We should follow the example of the Father of the Nation, Mahatma Gandhi, who would create magic by his use of simple and polite words. But there was firmness beneath his politeness and Gandhiji would convey the right message to the listener. So learn to be polite, but firm and keep a check on your anger. Such an attitude will save you from many unwanted problems.

24. A Lesson from a Beggar

For the really hungry, any food is sumptuous!

spoilt teenager of some rich parents was very fussy about the taste of food provided to him. Even a slight variation in the quantity of salt in his food would enrage him and he would throw away the food!

His mother tried her best to prepare food according to his taste and liking, but he would always find fault and blame the mother. Both the parents would try to pacify him, but he would mostly get angry

and refuse to eat. This made the parents very unhappy, while he himself remained dissatisfied.

One day, he and his parents had to go to the railway station to see off his newly married sister. As they were waiting at the station for the departure of the train, his eyes fell on a poor beggar, who was in rags and sitting behind a pillow with his torn bag. He saw the beggar taking out a cup from the bag. He filled his cup with water from the water tap at the station and came back to the same place. Then he took out a dried *chapatti* from his bag,. He would dip the *chapatti* in the cup of water, so that it can get soft and then eat it. In this way, the hungry beggar ate up the whole of the *chapatti*.

The boy watched the beggar, very carefully, while he was eating his *chapatti*. This incident stayed in his mind and he started thinking deeply. The picture of the beggar eating his dried *chapatti* calmly by dipping in tasteless water kept flashing in his mind. On the other hand, he had the luxury of rich tasty food of all sorts and still was angry and dissatisfied. That night, he quietly ate whatever was prepared for dinner, without getting angry and making any complaint. The boy got a lesson from the poor beggar. From that day, he became a changed person and never annoyed his parents with his rude behaviour.

25. A Matter of Faith

Mind Matters more than Holy Robes!

Once, a hermit (sanyasi) and a prostitute used to live in houses adjacent to each other. It so happened that both died on the same day. Lord YAMA's servants, who were sent to fetch them, were confused as to why they were asked to take the *sanyasi* to hell and the prostitute to heaven! But the mystery was removed later....

The order to shift the *sanyasi* to hell came despite his enjoying a good

reputation and the prostitute in ill fame because of her bad profession. Lord Yama's servants, or *Yamdoots* thought that there was some goof up! So they went to Chitragupta who was keeping all records for verification and guidance. Chitragupta verified and found that Lord YAMA'S orders were in order.

The fact was – their external appearances deceived the reality. Every morning when the *Sanyasi* used to chant the holy *mantras*, the prostitute living in the opposite house wanted to be present at the prayers, but could not do so because of her profession. So she would purify herself by crying out to remove her guilt. Since she yearned to participate in God's worship, she would put her ears against the walls of the *sanyasi's* house and fill herself with the holy thoughts of God sincerely praying that in her next life, she be given on opportunity to serve at a temple.

But the *sanyasi* had different thoughts. At night, when he would hear the sounds of dance and music in the opposite house, he would pity himself that he could not enjoy the pleasure there. So he cursed his lot as a *sanyasi* and longed to visit the house of the prostitute but could not do so because of his holy external garb!

So Chitragupta explained to the *Yamdoots* that in reality the *sanyasi* was living in a brothel and the prostitute lived in the temple because of their inner thoughts! So, it is the reality inside which matters and not the external appearances!

26. Gender Discrimination

Loving children on the basis of gender is a crime!

Men and women are equal. But as the topmost creation of God, both are complementary to each other. However, our society rejoices at the birth of a male child and considers it superior to a female. Why so? The following story will be an eye-opener!

The only grown up son of a rich man went abroad to settle there in search of greener pastures, without informing his father and only sister.

He sold his movable property and flew overseas, with his wife. His aged and sick father was left to the care of his married daughter, who had to shift to her father's house to look after him. About a year later, the father became seriously ill and was admitted to a private hospital, where he died soon. The son was informed, he rushed back, paid the bills and performed all the death rites and returned overseas.

Most people criticised the son for abandoning his father at his old age. It was the daughter who came to help her old father even at the cost of disrupting her settled life in another city! Despite several such incidents, the society rules a son more precious than a daughter as the son is supposed to carry forward the family name. What a travesty of our family structure, which we are boasting to the outer world! The fact is, it is high time we avoided gender discrimination to create a just and better society.

27. Teamwork

Teamwork cuts the tedium of work!

A man lost his way while driving through the countryside. In his effort to find the right way, he accidentally drove off the road and fell into a pit. His car was stuck deep in the mud, though he was not injured. He went over to a nearby farm and sought help. He had an interesting experience.

A farmer there agreed to come to his rescue. He said, "Yes, my old mule, WARWICK can help." So the two men with a mule came to the pit. The farmer hitched the mule to the car and shouted, "Pull Pull, JACK, Pull Brown, Pull WARWICK," and in a second, the car was pulled out.

The man thanked the farmer, patted the mule and enquired, "Tell me, why did you call the other two names, while only Warwick was there?" The farmer smiled and replied, "The old Warwick is blind. When I call the other two names, he thinks that he is working as a part of a team, so he does not have to pull alone."

Thus the spirit of teamwork leads to success. Sometimes, belief is all that you need to do a job and success is assured.

28. An Orphan and His Home

There is always a payback time!

Once, a three-month old abandoned baby was picked up by a team of young doctors, who ran an orphanage for poor children. From there, the child grew up and studied up to the high school. Unfortunately, the facilities at the home were turning worse due to the shortage of funds. How this misery affected that boy and how he addressed them is the crux of the story......

The young boy had a hard life in the orphanage. With the help of his other companions, he lodged a protest and fought for better facilities in the orphanage. Moved by their plight, the authorities provided funds and the conditions improved. The boy could not continue his studies as he had no means and therefore, sought employment in a bakery. Meanwhile, he also registered himself in the employment exchange. Sometime later, he was offered the job of a peon in the same orphanage, where he had spent his early childhood. He thought, it was an opportunity for him to improve the lot of children there. He worked hard and conditions improved. He loved and helped the children in all possible manner. Soon more children flocked to the same orphanage in view of the improved conditions. The abandoned child who was once brought as an orphan to the orphanage became the father figure to about 300 inmates. He volunteered to serve in the orphanage and made it his home as long as he lived.

29. The Satvik Food

According to the yogic texts, pure vegetarian food promotes love, purity and goodness, besides health and strength. That is why the practitioners of yogic culture and spiritual discipline are particular about what one should eat.

Such foods are called *satvik foods* which include fresh fruits, organic vegetables, whole wheat and pulses. Nuts, Intoxicants, cola, coffee, eggs, meat and strong spices are not included in this category.

Merely eating *satvik food* is not enough; the method of cooking should also be *satvik*. Deep frying should he avoided in any case. Cooking over low heat and steaming are better alternatives. *Satvik* principles also involve how to eat and how much to eat. Food should be chewed well and overeating should be avoided. *Satvik food* makes the mind clear and peaceful, and enables wisdom to flow freely and shine through the whole body. So *Satvik food* is the preferred food to nourish the mind and the soul.

30. The Importance of Shoulders in Human Body

Supportive attitude develops leadership skills!

Once a mother asked her son, "What is the most important part of a human body?" The son thought of sound as the most important to humans, and replied, "Ears." But the mother enlightened him with the right answer....

That was a wrong answer. After a while, she asked the same question to her son, who replied, "Our eyes, as sight is important to everybody." The answer was not correct. A few years later, her husband died and she cried placing her head on the shoulder of her young son, who was an adult by then.

She then asked the same question to her son, with tears rolling down her eyes. The son was very much surprised to hear that question on that sad occasion and he looked confused. The mother then told him, "The most important part of the body is the shoulder." He said: "Because it can hold the head." She said, "No, it is because it can hold the head of a grieving person or loved one when they cry. Son, in life, a time comes when everyone needs a shoulder to cry on."

It means one should be sympathetic to the pain of others, who will never forget your sympathy.

31. The Real Peace

Staying Calm amidst Turbulence is a Sign of Strength!

A King announced a hefty prize to an artist, who would paint the best picture of peace. Many artists tried their luck. But the outcome was interesting...

The King saw their pictures but shortlisted only two — one was that of a calm lake with peaceful towering hills around it and a blue sky full of

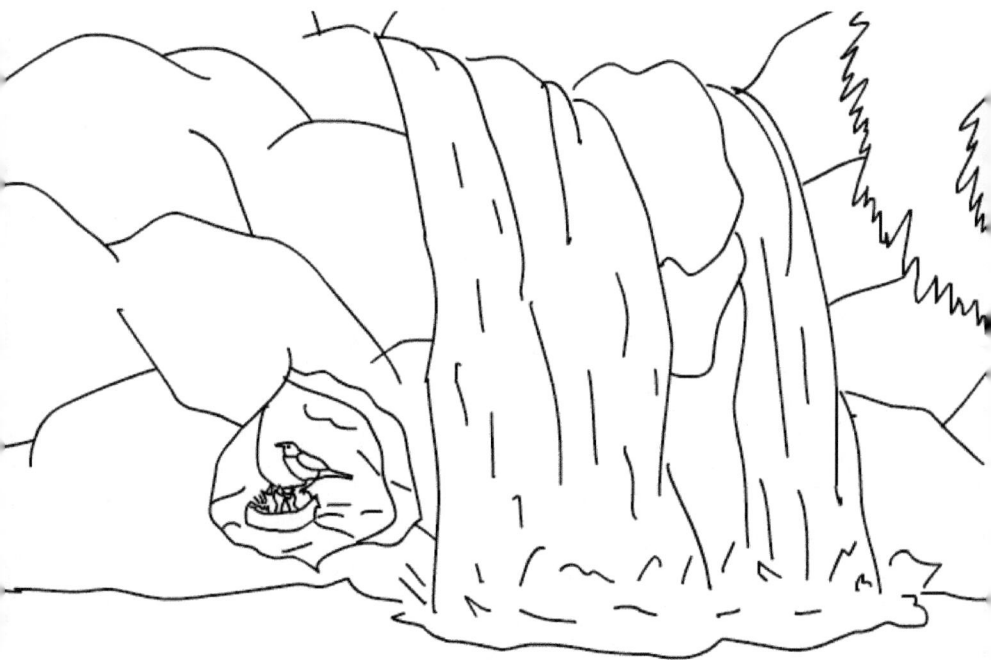

white clouds, overhead. The lake looked like a perfect mirror of peaceful surroundings.

The other picture also had mountains which were dry and rugged, with a turbulent sky overhead, lashing lightning and rain. A waterfall was making lot of noise down the mountainside. It was all a noisy scene. But, behind the waterfall was a rack with a small crack and inside it was a tiny bush. Inside the bush was a small mother bird, who built a nest and sat peacefully, unaware of the angry sky, noisy waterfall or disturbing environment. This presented a perfect picture of peace!

The King chose the second picture for prize! For him, peace meant staying calm at heart amidst all noises. It was the real meaning of PEACE – *the peace within*.

32. Thoughts of Kabir

Thoughts and words of great men always inspire us!

Kabir was a saint and one of India's greatest spiritual thinkers. As a social reformer, he tried to uplift the downtrodden and preached against useless religious rituals. He also tried to reconcile religious differences and advocated love and unity among all classes of society laying stress on honest, simple and spiritual life. He showed them the path of worship and salvation, and urged to shun orthodox practices and superstitions. Kabir expressed his thoughts in simple language and addressed the common man. Some of his profound thoughts are mentioned below for the benefit of the reader:-

When the body is burnt, it becomes ash
When it is not burnt, worms eat it up.
A soft clay vessel will break,
When water is poured into it
Such is the nature of the body.
Why, oh brother, just then puffing and blowing thyself out?
As the bee collects honey with great nest
So the fool collects wealth

When a man is dead, they say,
'Take him away! Take him away!
Why allow a ghost to remain?'
His wedded wife accompanies him to the door,
and after that his male friends
All other members of his family,
go up till the cremation ground,
The soul departs all alone.

Who is a Hindu? Who is a Turk?
Both inhabit the same earth
One reads the Vedas, the other the Quran.
One is a Maulana, the other a Pandit.
They are like earthen vessels,
Having different names but made of the same earth.
Both are misled and have not found God.
The external forces conceal from our eyes the deep meaning of existence,
True faith resides in the heart.

Long not for a dwelling in heaven,
And fear not to dwell in hell,
What will be, will be,
O my soul, hope not at all
Sing the praises of God
From whom the supreme reward is obtained.

Be not glad at the sight of prosperity,
And grieve not at the sight of adversity:
As is prosperity, so is adversity;
What God proposes shall be accomplished.

Some of Kabir's *dohas* in Hindi follows:-

Jahaan dayaa, wahaan dharm hai,
Jahaan lobh, tahaan paap
Jahaan krodh, wahan kaal hai,
Jahaan krishana, tahan aap.

It means kindness is the basis of true religion; greed is a sin and anger is the cause of destruction. Kabir says, to forgive is divine. In the following *doha*, Kabir advises us to cultivate humility:-

Kabira garv na keejiye, kaal gahe kar kes
Na jaane kit mare hai, kyaa des kyaa pardesh.

Do not nurture pride, as one does not know when and where one is destined to die.

In another *doha*, Kabir advises not to postpone one's work, as one does not know what will happen in the next moment:-

Kaal kare so aaj kar, aaj kare so aab
Pal main parley hojagi, bahuri karega kab.

Kabir advises against worry in the following *doha*:-

Chintaa aise daakini, kaat kalejaa khaaye
Baid heelaraa kija karey, kalan tak dava lagaay.

Worry is a silent killer and no medicine can cure it.

His masterpiece and popular *doha* is:-

Kabira khadaa bazaar main, maange sabki khair
Na kohon si dosti, no kohon se bair.

Kabir wishes welfare of all; he is neither friend nor foe to anybody.

In another *doha*, saint Kabir advises self-analysis and not to find faults in others. He says:-

Bura jo dekhan main chala
Bura na milia koye
Jo dil khoja aapna,
Mujsa bura na koye.

'When I went to find a bad person, I could not find any. However, when I looked within me, I thought no one was worse than me!' Thus we need not find faults in others, but look within ourselves and remove our own faults. In another *doha*, kabir points towards the insecurity and miseries of life and says:-

Chalti chakki dekh ke,
Diya kabira roye
Do patun kek beach main,
Sabut bacha na koye.

It means that nothing remains intact between the two grinding stones; life is all full of insecurity and miseries.

Aise vaani boliye,
Man ka aapa khoye,
Aapan ko sheetal kare,
Auron ko sukhe deye.

In this *doha*, Kabir advises us to speak gently without pride, ego and hatred. A sweet tongue not only calms our nerves, but gives a soothing effect to the listener.

Kabir gives a formula for leading a pure, peaceful life in the following *doha*:

Kabira man nirmal bhaya,
Jaisey ganga neera
Pachhey pachhey Hari phirey
Kahat Kabira Kabira

A simple and pure life without malice for any one keeps the mind clean and humble. In this pure state, God will always be with you.

33. The Wanderers

The nobler the blood, the less the pride

Two wanderers met on the sea beach. They had a friendly talk. One said to the other,

"At the high tide of the sea, long ago,
With the point of my staff,
I wrote a line, upon the sand

Which the people still pause to read
And they are careful
That none shall erase it!"

The other man said, "I too wrote a line upon the sand, but it was at low tide, and the waves of the sea washed it away. But tell me, what did you write?"

And the first man said, "I wrote, as follows:

I am he who is....

Now tell me what did you write?"

And the other man answered, I wrote this, "I am but a drop of the great ocean."

—KHALIL GIBRAN

34. Thank God - For Your Blessings

ost of us in this material world do not count the blessings in our life and mourn only about the losses. Is there a good way to be more positive in life?

The important thing is to count on our blessings and thank God for what he has given us, and convert the losses into gains. God has given us numerous blessings and CONTENTMENT is the top of all. It all depends on our mental attitude and how we react to the happenings in our life. The following two lives provide some guidance:-

"Two men looked out of the prison bars,
One saw the mud, the other saw stars."

This is how the right attitude makes a difference! We must enjoy the good things which happen to us and be grateful to our creator instead of grumbling about unsavoury and sad things. It will be relevant to quote great poet GOETHE in the following lines:

"My crown is in my heart, not on my head;

Not decked with diamonds and Indian stones;

 Not to be seen, my crown is called CONTENT.

A crown it is that seldom kings enjoy."

These lines nicely indicate the value of contentment. We may, briefly, mention our many blessings in life, which are common to most of us, as follows:

1. Our body and good health
2. The house where we live
3. Our life partner
4. The children
5. Free air that we breathe and without which we cannot live and the life standing water and sunshine.
6. Our food and clothing
7. Good company and good friends and relatives
8. The forests, the green grass and plants
9. The starry blue sky at night
10. The clouds, the rain which brings life and joy
11. The change in seasons
12. All good opportunities in our life
13. Faith, hope and courage and all good qualities which make life noble and nice
14. The peace of mind and inner strength

We should count these blessings and many more, and thank God for his love and kindness.

35. A Fight Against All Odds

Tales of Heroes can do wonders in moments of distress!

*T*his is the story of a brave woman, who fought all odds and bounced back to life. It was an accident which nearly made her immobile for a couple of years. But she recovered. How?

It was possible only because of her determination and the loving care of her parents. Their motto was, "It does not matter what happens

to you. What really matters is how you react to it." This was her earliest lesson in survival.

A few years later, as a result of a freak incident at an office party, she was hospitalised on the ground of permanent hearing loss. In the hospital, she could see doctors and nurses talking, but could not hear their voices. In spite of all sorts of treatment and medication, there was no cure. But she had received great support from the hospital staff, parents and relatives. She had learnt from her voracious reading as to how brave people had overcome great challenges in life including disabilities, with grit and determination.

She fought her battle hard, drawing inspiration from the stories she read. With the help of sophisticated hearing aids and help extended by colleagues along with the loving care received from parents, she got back to work and started doing well. What an amazing success story!

36. Tit For Tat - A Lesson For Life

Ungrateful behaviour precedes untold miseries!

This is the story of an aged person, who was maltreated by his young sons. In our modern age, youngsters consider their elderly parents as great nuisance and grown up children often try to ignore them. A bitter father, who was at the receiving end of such a humiliation decided to give a fitting reply to his selfish sons. What was his plan?…

A retired person spent all his savings to build a big house. He had wife and three young sons. He gave one floor each to his sons, and lived with his eldest son at the ground floor, along with his wife. A few years

later, his wife expired and he became totally dependent on his eldest son for his food and daily needs. One day, this son complained that his other two brothers were not contributing to the upkeep of their father. So it was decided that the father would stay with each family, turn by turn, for an equal period. But this arrangement did not work out and the helpless father started taking his meals at a nearby *dhaba*.

This was not a satisfactory arrangement for the father. His old friends, realising his plight hatched a plan to teach a lesson to his sons who ill-treated their father. One day the father called his three sons and gave them tickets for a fully paid holiday for a month. They were very happy to accept this offer and went on a vacation with their families. When they returned, they found a builder in their house, who asked the sons to take away their belongings and vacate the house as it had been sold to him by their father. They were also shocked to know that their father had left for an unknown destination without leaving any contact address. This was the fitting reply the old father gave to his sons for the maltreatment and humiliation heaped on him!

Human beings make the mistake of becoming too attached to their family and worldly possessions. They come to grief when they feel rejected by their own people. It is therefore, essential to train our minds in spiritual pursuits and develop an affinity towards God, so that we do not feel lonely and neglected in the old age. Sri Ramakrishna said, "The best way to live life is to live like a caretaker. A caretaker does not maintain any attachment for his possessions and remains calm even if they are snatched away from him."

37. Forty Years Together

The heart that truly loves never forgets!

A husband and wife had a long married life. One night, the wife found her husband missing from their bed. She got up to look for him and found him sitting in the dining room with moist eyes. She watched him and said, "Dear, what is the matter? What are you doing here?"

The husband said, "Do you remember when we were dating 40 years ago?" The wife, touched by her husband's concern said. "Yes, I remember. I was only 18 then."

The husband then said haltingly, "Do you remember when your father caught us making love behind the couch? The wife came closer and said, "Yes, I remember." The husband then said, "Do you remember how he pointed his revolver on my face and shouted, "Either you marry my daughter or be ready to go to jail for 40 years." His wife replied very gently, "Yes, I remember all that." Then the man, wiping tears from his cheeks said, "If that happened, I would have got out today!"

38. Lost to Win

Sacrifice is a jewel that will shine throughout a life time and beyond!

This is the story of an ace sportsman--a table tennis player, who won a match but got himself declared as a loser in order to help another needy player to get a job. But that does not put full stop to his success...

A sportsman applied for the post of an engineer and as per rules, he had to win a match against others to qualify. When he won the match, the referee came to him and made him agree to be declared as a loser as his opponent needed that job badly, in view of his adverse financial condition. He had to support his mother, sisters and younger brother, and his father had expired a week ago. This sportsman who sacrificed his job in favour of another person soon got another good job. There he worked hard and rose high in the career after getting quick promotions. He also won all India championships for his company and brought honour for himself.

By losing the winnable match to favour a needier person for a job, this sportsman showed his large-heartedness. This kind gesture further reinforced his success and prosperity in later life in another well-deserved manner!

39. The Great Illusion

Dangers of self-love and illusions of true love!

A Guru had a disciple who was a householder. He used to advise his disciple to renounce the world and join him to attain the highest goal in life. The disciple was reticent. See how the Guru played an interesting episode in his life…

The disciple used to say, "Sir, how can I leave my affectionate parents, loving wife and children?" The Guru said, "All these are mere illusion. I will show you the reality." The Guru then gave a pill to the disciple to swallow. After taking the pill, the disciple became still like a corpse but did not lose his consciousness.

Following this development, the members of the disciple's house were overcomed by grief and all were wailing. Hearing the loud cries, a holy man appeared on the scene, who saw the dead body and touched it. Then he said, "I have a medicine which can bring him back to life. But another person has to die in his place." Surprisingly, for the young man, nobody was ready to die and all the relatives excused themselves on some pretext or another. The affectionate parents said, "We have to look after the big household." The loving wife said, "I have to look after my small children." The disciple was hearing everything and he got up suddenly and touched the feet of the holy man, who was none else, but his Guru. The disciple then said, "Sir, I will follow you. Let us go."

40. Face of Humility

It is easy to find faults in others, but difficult to look for it within oneself!

A man, after realising that he was a great sinner, went to a holy person and said, "Sir, I am a great sinner. Please advise, as to how I can be saved. The holy man said, "Go and find out a greater sinner than you are, or bring something which is worse than you."

He went away, looked around, but could not find anything worse than him! Then a thought came to him, as he saw his own excrement

and said, "Surely, this is something worse than me." So he wanted to pick it up and take it to the holy man. As soon as he stretched his hands, he heard a voice from the rubbish "O sinner, how come you think me worse than you." I was a delicious pudding pleasing to all. Due to my misfortune, I was reduced to this horrible condition, when you ate me up. So do not touch me again for further degradation!" Hearing this, the man learnt a lesson in true humility and attained the highest stage of perfection.

41. Practical Lesson

A Good Leader always leads from the front!

This is an interesting story of a school principal who literally tried to lead the students by examples. He demonstrated how not to waste food. What did he do to send his message that was loud and clear!

One day, he visited the hostel mess, where the students had just finished their lunch. There, he was shocked to see a lot of leftover food

in several plates lying on the table. He called up all the students and in their presence, ate the leftover food from one plate. Then he gave a pep talk about the food shortage and the starving millions, below the poverty line, in our country. He impressed upon the students to take as much food in their plates, as they actually needed and not to waste any food. The above practical lesson of the principal had a great effect on the students, who took the vow in his presence, not to waste any food, in the future.

42. Consequence of Fear

A brave man dies only once but a coward dies a million times!

A philosopher was walking in a garden and felt something following him. When he looked back, there was none but a shadow. It was death!

The philosopher questioned the shadow: "Who are you and where

are you going?" The shadow muttered: "I am the spectre of death and I am going to fetch a hundred dead bodies." Saying this, it disappeared.

Next day, that place was hit by plague and a thousand people died. The same philosopher, while walking in the garden met the shadow of death and asked, "You told me that you were going to fetch a hundred dead bodies, but in the town one thousand people have died. How do you explain this?"

Death replied, "That is not my fault. I got only one hundred persons, but the nine hundred died only out of fear of dying!"

This is the result of fear. We should not lose our confidence and live life without fear.

43. Unnecessary Worry

Live in the moment and be happy!

A rich man amassed so much of wealth that another seven generations could enjoy it. Still he was unhappy and had a worried look. Subsequently, he fell ill. On being quizzed by his wife, the man finally revealed his cause of worry. What was it?

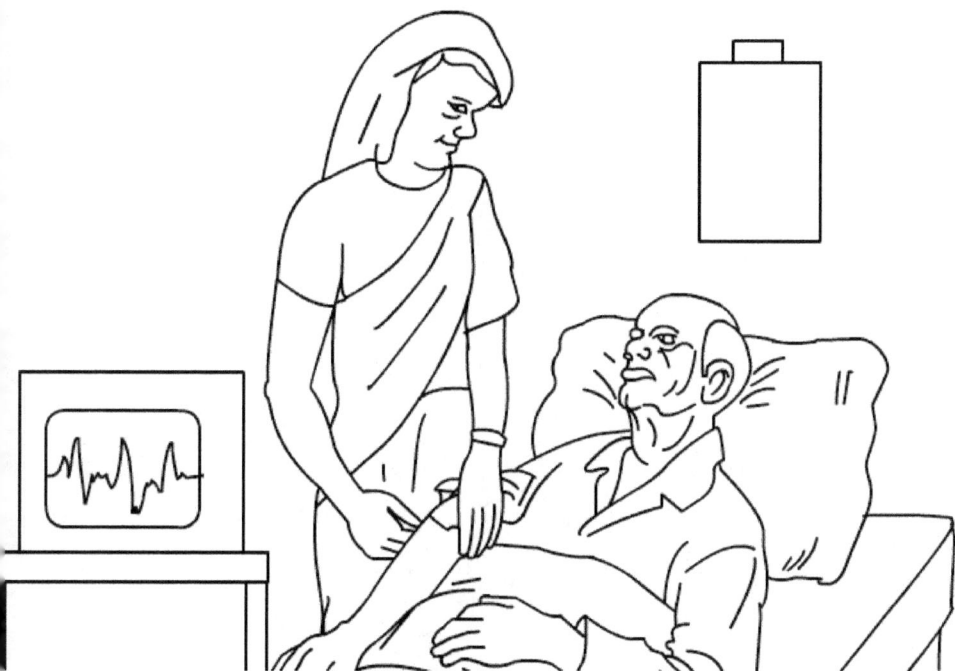

His wife asked him, "Your illness is due to your worry. Please tell me, what makes you worry? You have everything and there is hardly any reason for your anxiety." The rich man thought for a while and said, 'Yes I have everything and much more so that our seven generations can live on that." His wife intervened to say, "Then, what is bothering you?" he said, "Oh, but I am worried about the 8th generation?!"

This is a glaring example of unnecessary worry. We should take care of our present and need not worry much spoiling our future.

44. A Story of Broken Trust

Chicanery Gets Hard Lashing!

A famous Sufi saint set out on a long journey accompanied by his disciples. When they were feeling tired and hungry, they took rest under the shade of a tree which had a bunch of birds perched on its branches. Then the animal instincts of one of his disciples worked and that led to an unpleasant situation…

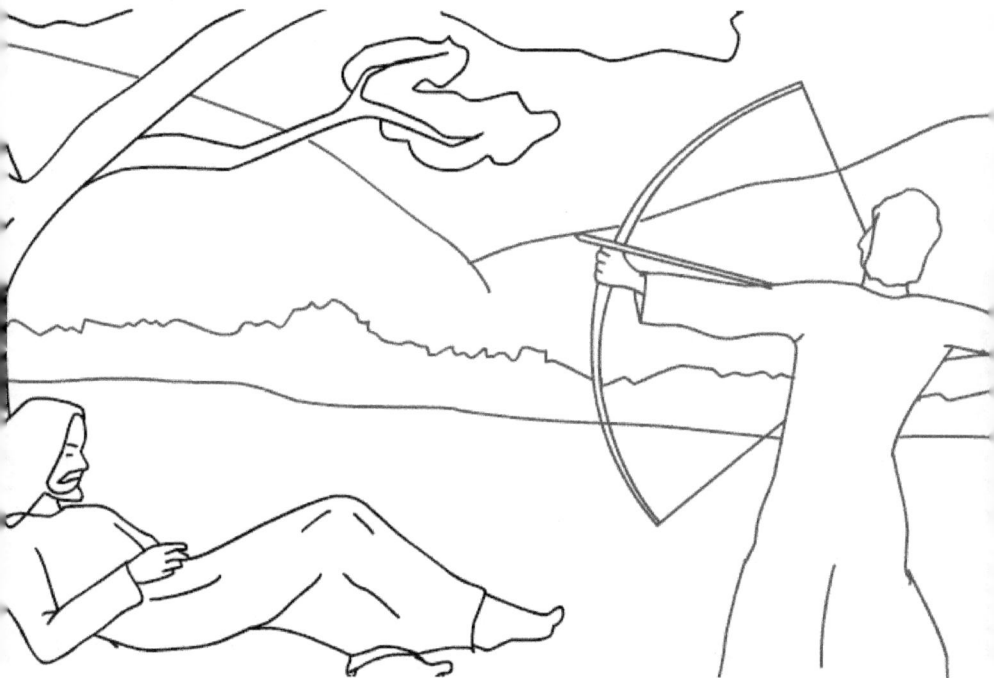

One of the disciples of the saint took out his bow and arrow and killed one bird as a supplement to their food. At this, other birds started croaking and making noise which attracted the attention of the Sufi, who, using his spiritual powers, talked to the leader of the birds and enquired the reason for their unusual croaking. The head bird said they wanted justice for the killing of one of their team-mates. The Sufi pulled up the disciple and asked for an explanation for his cruel act. The disciple tried to excuse himself saying that he committed no offence as hunting was permitted. The head bird reacted by saying, "As Sufis are harmless people, we were not scared. If you were common people, we would have flown away, so you have deceived us."

The Sufis thought over this and agreed that even though hunting was allowed, the disciple had broken the trust of these unsuspecting birds. The accused was, therefore adjudged guilty and given a severe punishment.

45. How Little Things Matter

Even Small Steps make a Difference!

nce a man was walking along a beach and noticed another man repeatedly picking up something from the ground and throwing it into the sea. He decided to check it out.....

The man who was looking at this became curious and came closer to see what the other man was doing. He was actually picking up small

fish and hurling them into the sea. These fish had been washed ashore by the sea waves and could not go back to the sea water. He asked the other man why he was doing that. The other man replied, "I am throwing them back into the water to save them." The first man said, "Yes, I know, there are thousands of small fish on the beach. Throwing back a few would not make much difference."

That man smiled picking up another fish and throwing it back to the water and said, "This will surely make a difference at least to that one!"

And he was right. Even little things matter!

46. Unwanted Desires

Too much of pampering can play spoilsport!

A man had a pet dog, which he loved very much. The pampered dog in turn would play funny games and poke pranks at its master. Finally, the master decided to mend the ways of the pet dog in a novel way.

One day, a learned man came to his house and both sat down for a chat. All of a sudden the dog came and jumped into the lap of the master, licking his cheek. The visitor did not like it and expressed his displeasure to the house owner, and admonished him for pampering the dog so much. This had the desired result; the man decided to teach a lesson to the dog. Every time the dog would jump to lick his face, it was given a kick. The dog was quick to learn and changed its habit, improved and behaved well, thereafter.

Similarly, our unwanted desires are like a pampered pet trying to overwhelm us. Proper control in the form of repeated blows and counter thoughts can cure them.

47. Good and Bad Turns

Forget and forgive must be the philosophy of all good persons!

Two friends were walking through a desert. During the journey, they quarrelled over a dispute and one friend slapped the other. The one, who was slapped wrote on the sand, "Today my best friend slapped me." He was hurt, but did not say anything. His logic was edifying...

As they walked on, they came to an oasis, where they decided to take bath. Unfortunately, the one who got slapped, got stuck in the mud and was about to get drowned. However, the other saved him and brought him out of the pool. The person, who was saved, engraved on the stone "Today, my best friend saved my life." The other enquired, "When I hurt you, you wrote on sand. But now, when I saved you, you engraved it on the stone. Please explain this."

The other friend said: "When someone hurts you, you should forget it soon, like a writing on the sand gets blown away. But if someone does you good, try to remember it long, like the engraving on stone that cannot be blown away.

48. Human Life is Precious

An elephant never knows its strength!

When a diamond merchant died, he bequeathed a rare and invaluable diamond to his wife. One day she sent out her younger son to the market to know and verify the market value of the diamond but advised him against selling it. He heard many prices from many merchants. Then…

First he took it to a vegetable seller, who offered some potatoes in exchange. Then he went to a shopkeeper, who offered a hundred rupees. Then he took it to a goldsmith, who valued it at two thousand rupees. A diamond merchant was prepared to give ten thousand rupees. At last he came to know about a man, who was an expert in rare and precious diamonds; so he asked his opinion. The man said that the diamond was worth many millions of rupees and was invaluable.

This story is an allegory of human life itself which is priceless. It depends how a person uses it and values it. Majority of human beings do not realise the true value of life and waste it in useless pursuits. Human life is priceless; it is a rare gift from the God. It should he used properly to realise its best possible value by focussing on noble causes.

49. Acceptance of Existence

Accepting God in broad humility!

This is the story of a Sufi mystic by the name, Junnaid who would express his gratitude to God for his existence, and the love, care and compassion bestowed on him. Once Junnaid and his companions set out on a journey and they starved without food for three days continuously. The outcome was a lesson to all…

They did not get any food and water from the villages they crossed. Thinking that his teachings were bad and selfish, the villagers shunned him and refused to help. On the third day, Junnaid and his followers were in great trouble. His disciples began to murmur and said, "Now let us see how he expresses his gratitude for his existence and what does he say in his prayers?"

When the time of prayers came, Junnaid said his prayers as usual, expressing deep gratitude to the God. After the prayer, the disciples started grumbling and said: "This is not tolerable. We have been suffering from thirst and hunger for the last three days! We have not even slept and all are tired. Here you are still thanking God for your existence and telling that it takes care and is very compassionate!"

Junnaid heard this and said: "My prayer does not depend on any condition which is of ordinary nature. Whether I get food or not, I won't blame my existence. They are only small things in this vast universe. It won't matter to me if I don't get food and water and even if I die. I will pray in the same manner. It hardly makes any difference to this vast universe whether Junnaid is dead or alive!"

The above story shows how life should be accepted by all. Life is not obliged to fulfil all our desires; it gives us what we deserve. Acceptance of life as it is will give us satisfaction and happiness. For a truly religious person, acceptance of whatever life brings is real PRAYER!

50. The Value of Truth

One more experiment with truth!

About 1000 years ago, in Iraq, there was a child named Abdul Qadir. One day he heard a voice urging him to undertake his greatest mission in life. He felt inspired and told his mother that he wanted to go to Baghdad to pursue higher education. The mother agreed and gave him an important advice…

She granted him permission to go, but stitched 40 gold coins inside his coat's lining, and said. "Oh, my son, since you are going, I shall bear the separation from you for the service of God. But do follow my advice--always feel the truth, speak the truth and propagate the truth, even at the risk of your life."

Qadir heard his mother carefully and promised to follow her advice; Come what may! On the way to Baghdad, he was attacked by robbers. He honestly told them about the gold coins hidden in his coat. When the robbers found them, the robbers were astonished and the leader asked Qadir what prompted him to reveal the hidden treasure. Qadir said: "My mother had advised me to speak the truth even at the risk of my life. I promised her to follow her advice. That is why I told you the truth." The robbers were impressed by his sincerity and felt remorseful from that day onwards and gave up robbing people and began a good life, afresh.

That small child was only eight years old when he left home to pursue knowledge and later became a great saint, who was known as Sheikh Abdul Qadir Gelani. He followed his mother's advice; practised truth and became a saintly scholar and social reformer.

It is said that Truth is God or God is truth. We should always live by the truth.

51. The Great President

A Noble Soul never ceases to delight and comfort!

During the American civil war, Abraham Lincoln, the famous President of the U.S.A. visited hospitals to cheer the injured soldiers. Thus he came across an injured soldier, who was on his death bed. The President asked him, "Is there anything I can do for you?" He had a curious request....

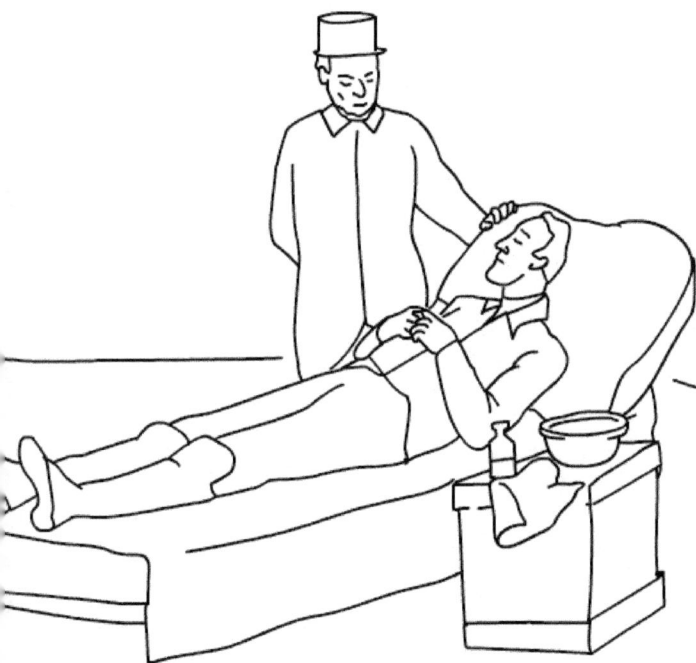

The soldier, without knowing the identity of the visitor, said, "Please write a letter to my old mother." The President sat beside him to take the dictation. The soldier said, "Dear mother, I have been fatally injured, while fighting for my country and shall die shortly. Do not grieve for me. May God bless you." Lincoln closed the letter with a postscript "written for your son by Abraham Lincoln." When the soldier saw the letter, he was greatly astonished that his visitor was none else but the President himself. Lincoln again enquired, "Is there anything else, I can do for you?" The young man said, "Please hold my hand so that I can die peacefully."

The kind President obliged and the soldier died in peace. Even small compassionate deeds matter a great deal.

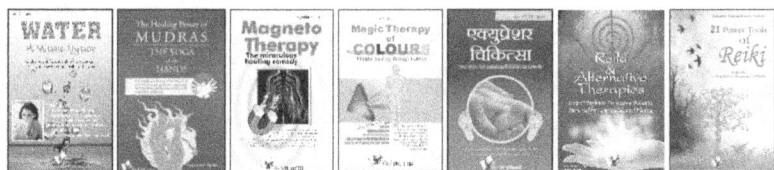